T0128890

Pretty Eyes
Ugly Cries

Pretty Eyes Ugly Cries

TAMEEKA SPATES

PRETTY EYES UGLY CRIES

iUniverse books may be ordered through booksellers or by contacting:

iUniverse
1663 Liberty Drive
Bloomington, IN 47403
www.iuniverse.com
1-800-Authors (1-800-288-4677)

ISBN: 978-1-5320-7317-5 (sc)
ISBN: 978-1-5320-7318-2 (e)

Print information available on the last page.

iUniverse rev. date: 04/12/2019

Pretty Eyes, Ugly Cries

"Bring the tissues; face the issues"

There are many descriptors of an ugly cry, but most are associated with pain. One may have experienced an ugly cry in a movie due to a bad break up portrayed by an actor, one of his/her very own, and or through a betrayal of a close friend. However, another may have experienced an ugly cry due to the loss or death of a love one. Although, it has been said that break-ups can feel like a death, not every heartbreak warrants the same cure. One may choose to party like a rockstar, drink away his/her blues; while another may replace the old with a new or choose to invest his/her time and energy into something or someone to aid and block from the hurt. When it comes to the matter of the heart we feel the attack is brief and short lived. We are then expected to get over it on someone else's time. We fail to understand that grief doesn't have an end date and must realize that every heartbreak isn't the same.

Therefore, ugly cries may not only consists of tears, but an attitude or an emotion evoked from pain and the fear of reliving that pain again if we dare open up. Just think, to die spiritually or literally? For example, think of an open or closed casket; does it really matter to someone who's claustrophobic, but are no longer physically here on earth? When a spirit is trapped by fear it's restricted and once it's freed nothing can contain it. The example shows how one may choose to define death. By being guarded, we think we're fixing the problem placing a brick wall or barb wire around our hearts. Instead, we must take caution and never allow pain to get pent up and stored. We should at least attempt to free ourselves by removing one brick at a time and be cautious during any tantrums not to throw these same stones that bricked us in at others who dare to come close.

If we choose to embrace the ugly cries, it may rinse away the debris from our eyes, relieve the hurt and guard from infection. Ugly cries may leave us to feel we are drowning in a sea of resentment, anger, bitterness, and debilitate us from feeding our hunger pains for true love. Spiritually, ugly cries aid in detoxing the soul and frees one from death.

Summary

"***Pretty Eyes, Ugly Cries***" is a collection of poems in the style of Storytelling, Spoken Word, and Lyric Poetry. The writings describe a "spitfire" personality and are filled with raw emotions packed with entertainment. Each poem captures a certain attitude of a character. The style and language seek for deliberation; shuts out denial, and opens up the door to welcoming and entertaining inner peace. Throughout the collections, we find that pain begets tears and that tears are a crucial part in the soul cleansing process. We must understand that wounds are more than skin deep and recognize that true healing begins when we allow them to air out. Although, pain may come from removing the shield, the "Band-Aid", we learn this pain should be welcomed and not shunned in order for proper healing to take place. ***Pretty Eyes, Ugly Cries*** gather the true beauty of one's tears throughout the pain process. It shows one that they can overcome obstacles and will remain pretty once they've released a pretty ugly cry when stricken by an overflow of joy.

Pretty Eyes, Blue Contacts

Despite feeling blue from the many stones thrown her way...she collected, she sashayed; she exuded beauty

- Diamond in the Rough
- Hear Me In Private
- Pretty Ugly Cries
- A Rose Amongst Thorns
- Wondering Woman
- Beautiful Disaster
- Uncaptured Butterfly
- Name Changer
- Broken Wing
- Mirror Image
- Mind Reader
- Pain Re-liver
- Naked Butt Afraid
- Abandoned
- Promiscuity
- Out of Style
- Dying
- I'm Fine

Pretty Eyes Overshadowed Tear Jerkers

She smized; smiled with her eyes because she simply refused to become blind to the truth...

- All for Chance
- False See
- Boys Versus Men
- Mannequin
- Mad Dog
- Male Function
- Suited
- Mr. Comfortable
- Love's Prisoner
- Manipulators
- ICU
- Fly Trap
- Brainiac
- Melination
- Silence
- Enabler
- Puzzled
- Kin-Dred

Pretty Eyes Wiped Away Her Fears

She decided to wing it, tears smudged her liner;
she reapplied and drew the line,
she decided to fly

- Love Rollercoaster
- Love Defined
- The Couple
- The Wait
- Stagnant
- Let Go
- Love Me
- This Skin
- See Level
- Reclaim the Max
- Whole Some`one`
- Leaf
- The Truth
- So Low/Soul Low/Solo
- Ocean Floor
- Love In The Making
- Dear Husband
- Heroine

Contents

"Pretty Eyes Wiped Away Her Fears"

"Pretty Eyes, Blue Contacts"

Diamond in the Rough

Rough exterior, beautiful interior
Wrapped around your finger have you feeling superior
Although she's tough and hard to break
The refinery process not for the average who so easily crack; putting lives at stake
Often test bitten and tried to see if fake
Endures it all to shine so brightly sensitive eyes can't take
She's a cut above the rest, keep locked away and safe
So many attempt to steal and try to imitate
Pure carbon no carbon copy, polished attitude "icy" cold
The pressures placed upon a stoned rich soul
Diamond in the rough; a precious gem you cherish to have and hold
When you rock her you must be bold

Hear Me in Private

You say you listen
But you don't hear me though
I speak clearly
I speak purposefully
I speak to you in so many ways
The language of love
I never signed with my hands
So I began to wave
Boi Bye,
Seems that you never hear a word that I say
Somehow you only feel me whenever we lay
Oh, but my voice is so loud
My voice is so powerful, so powerful
For that smile, you can't see the frown plastered on my face
So focused on cutting the pie and winning the pie eating contest
Failed to notice you won in the first place
Clean the wax out your ears
Instead of focusing on waxing some
Ask me how I'm feeling, what I need and come through
Don't grab me from behind, rubbing your stick on my spine
With the door barely cracked, prying, trying to poke in; the candy shops'
closed no longer open
You will no longer feel me in private
For the sign on the entrance reads
Do not disturb

Pretty Ugly Cries

Pretty Eyes' bares all truth

Tear drops from her ugly cries are the proof

Her eyes glare, caught mid stare yet still she's flattering like the mascara she wears

A true covergirl, so dope so deep; loves to stay hidden most label her kind the black sheep, an outcast who's forbidden

With her makeup being so strong; heavy eye shadow covers her lid

She's left to question, "What I did?"

She answers herself without a blink

No one cares is what she thinks

She sinks in the corner with her head bowed to her knees

The salt water trickle from her ducts; her makeup bleeds

Despite the cold world, she continues to wear her heart on her sleeve

The despair, she wants to disappear; the agony can be felt through her gasps for air

Waterproof smeared liner, from wiping her face; she longs for a happy place

Pretty Eyes realize that her ugly cries release the sadness trapped inside, she manages to live; to survive

Unlike her makeup, she'll sparkle and shine

In her heart, she knows all will be fine

Her tears; may pour like rain

She's sure the "Son's" light will shine bright despite the pain

She'd overcome so much abuse, all of the attempts to rob her of her worth failed and was put to good use

A Rose Amongst Thorns

She's wrapped; covered
The color of blood
When she opens up; she blossoms
She's beautiful in nature and full of love
Although she's surrounded by thorns
She's quite the romantic gift flower, the most adorned
Seems complicated, yet she's purely simple
To touch her, use caution, be genuine be gentle

Wondering Woman

Those who are afraid have nothing to offer
Lost and confused, never kneeled before the altar
Their walk is staggering, they stay throwing tantrums; acting terrible twos
Cry the blues place value in their shoes
Don't waste your time and energy trying to figure them out
You can give them your heart, they'll still cast doubt
Want a woman they don't deserve
Play the victim, they have some nerve
Want to be crowned, no laughing matter; their clowns
How will they ever hold you tight, when they can't keep it together to hold you down?
Not literally, but figuratively speaking
They'll never be able to find you when it's themselves they're seeking
Take them at face value, don't be full of wonder
Fool for thought no more need to ponder

Beautiful Disaster

The quiet before the storm
The sound of sirens, the ringing of alarms
Wanting to ride it out, putting yourself at harm
Situation so unpredictable and you've been warned
Shaking up your world, ripping it apart
A vacant house without a roof, without a tarp
Far from tropical, no sunshine just rainy, cloudy; cold days
The doppler effect, categorizing of emotions; feelings from those hits, the surge crashing waves
Destroying & demolishing you for sure
So guarded & boarded up, no walking down the aisle; ransacked, like an empty shelf in a store
The tumultuous downpour
So broken you opened up like the sky
Tears fall like rain, due to the pain it's a constant cry
Flooding river banks now pose a threat
You're captured in the eye of the storm; beautiful disastrous effect

Un-Captured Butterfly

A beautiful thing that must remain
You seek to capture but can't contain
Breathtaking, it's clear
You just stop and stare
So beautiful, yet fragile handle gently with care
It's amazing, God's creativity
So stunning far from the caterpillar that use to be
No hiding in the chrysalis free to be shown, wings purposed to fly and
to roam

Name Changer

The day I had an epiphany
Dude asked my name
Told him it was Tiffany
I began to wonder because, I couldn't understand
The reason "Shun" tae & Roxanne didn't have a man
So much for first impression when I couldn't give my first name
Oh, how shit changed, when they switched up the game
Asked for my number, thought about…
Nowadays they have Google Maps; aside that, I possibly could be tracked, this dude could be whack
Something like a serial killer, serial dater & or mentally insane
On another note, I considered it all a joke, maybe just maybe he wanted to give me a ring
Instead of blowing out my brains, I'm for sure he hoped my back
Wasn't really my type, but y'all know the saying opposites attract
So, I gave him the digits 1-800-C/H/A-R/I/T/Y that's Charity
When it didn't add up, he asked for clarity
In addition to having him chase, I need someone who would fund my trust
To love, to cherish, to operate spiritually; not lust
This private profit organization brings about healing, stability, & relieve frustrations
If he'd put in the work; after all, he opted to volunteer his time
My true identity will be exposed, I'd lay it all on the line
Hi, I'm Joy, your heavenly Angel
I'm your Sunshine cause that's what I bring you

Broken Wing

The injury,
Seems that it will never heal
Hard pill to swallow, can't spread your wings to fly; life can get real
Fear spills over, Buzzards await you like road kill
The black tar, the situation; the turmoil
You toil
Why you wanna fly blackbird?
When you are feeling blue; question sounds absurd
Life's been robbing, you humm
Plagued by death, not in your nature to run, but you ran far away from
the nest
Yet you are hopeful keeping your eyes to sky, burdened without rest
Singing, "I Believe I Can Fly"
Feasted and preyed upon by hawks
Feeling caged, no parakeet, hate to repeat; if only these walls could talk
The taste of freedom lies in the breeze
Pigeon held, tired of being squeezed
The storms, the weather, not belonging to a flock
Vision of an Eagle instead of seagulls on the dock
Tweedle dee, tweedle dumb
Got injured, turned numb
Sea of emotions, refuse to drown
The watching eye stays on the sparrow
Shielding & protecting from the arrows
The sky so spacious, yet seems narrow
Once down; a wounded bird is out of place on the ground
Don't give up & die
Even when you're sore, soar just fly

Mirror Image

When I look in the mirror, I see a very familiar face
The one with her feelings, so far out of reach and misplaced
She looks a lot like myself, but there's something off
She tries to give me her hard heart, she knows mine is soft
She doesn't like who I am, to others I exude strength
She rather trade in her abused soul, wants me to forsake my confidence
The attempts to manipulate and tear down
Her tears, her sorrows she wants me to feel; she wants me to drown
This makeup is so heavy, I tried to wipe it off; cloth after cloth, but the remover didn't work
The dirt she attempted to throw didn't cover my worth
Got a little blind-sided, she wasn't far but near
We locked eyes, deep in stare
That warning, "objects seem closer than they appear"
It's no stranger, so I turn a deaf ear
The inner me, knows the enemy wants to conquer; to destroy
My reflection to make pretty; the ploy
I just simply refuse to let her still my joy

Mind Reader

Complacent, now your distant
So resistant the contentment
Got you resenting what you've been missing
No commitment, now your dissing
After all that you've be wishing
You've been on a crucial mission, to find a love loss
Just keep swinging at the toss
The moment you realize you need a boss
Yearning for the real, despise the false
Learning what's fake to avoid mistakes
Taken for granted done took all you could take
Tired of feeling walked on like dirt
Done having your feelings hurt
Dust them losers shake them off,
Stay focused and on course, dry those tears no remorse
No Rigor mortis, allow your heart to be soft
Ash the old flames, soon you'll forget their names
If they were hot, you wouldn't be so cold
Take my hand, let me show you what the future holds

Pain Re-Liver

I tried to ease the pain
To relieve the pain, I reached for the bottle
The medication wasn't enough
The side effects made my insides feel as if they were about to erupt
Due to pressures & depression from so much hurt, I needed to regurgitate;
I needed to just throw it up
I had pain trapped; covered
Finally discovered, that I was in need of an open-heart procedure
No love for me, felt huh, I didn't need you
My heart was bleeding, I was heated a spontaneous combustion
It was a must, I was closed in
From within my cries were muffled, my tears were silent
The confinement without commissary, I was a prisoner of pain
They say pain could be a good thing, it tells you when something's wrong
Masking could result in harm; danger
The cure; the wrapping of loving arms to apply pressure to help release the anger
I yearned for relief, through my belief, I would find inner peace
I thought…
When you're numb you can't feel & when you're pained you can heal
Got to be real with yourself, there's no plastic for this kind of surgery
Cause when going through your trial and tribulations lying just makes you commit perjury and put you in a closed in space; lock behind bars

If you must scream; shout do whatever it takes to get it out
Restore order in your life don't be held in contempt, get past don't resent
You may one day stare in a mirror, look through the windows at your soul,
to find it's empty; you've been devoured swallowed whole by bitterness &
unforgiveness
I had to stop crying from wounds that were old
I refused to die in pain; I refused to become cold

Naked Butt Afraid

Comfortable staying covered up
Contemplating a nip; tuck
Trying to get warm from the charm
Rather stay fully dressed had to many false alarms
Shivering yet barring all your soul, scared to be judge
A broken heart, the scars, the marks, that noticeable pudge
Besides giving birth not understanding your worth
You've opened up, regretting, not feeling bold
Show off-assuming courage too quick you got cold
Accepting the fact that your no playmate, model, and no centerfold
Keeping it real isn't ideal; the ideal image is being fake
Your feeling nervous, stretched, and a little bent out of shape
Weighing in the corner, you're the true mvp; a heavy weight
In this attempt to find comfort in your own skin
Close the door on fear, just show the beauty within

Abandoned

Birthed, left for dead, thoughts plaguing my head
A slow death, the agony wanting to belong, wanting to be
Why can't anyone just love me? Why?
Can they see me? Why can't they see me?
Left in the dust and although dirt I will return
Just my whole life feeling like dung covered in dirt; yet I still yearn
The feeling of being left on a doorstep, at the fire station, the trash
I express myself, I curse the generation, the pain sometimes burns; remains of ash
Product of prostitution, statistics say there's no resolution
I'm heading to an institution; when will I learn?
Some love child, victim of a wild lifestyle, was my mom to my dad just a piece of ass?
Abandonment issues cried so long from the misuse
The tissues soiled with tears and my fears of never belonging had become crystal clear; more like stained glass
Everyone comes then goes, feeling all bottled up like pop
A convenience store; an ez-serve, quick pit stop
Broken over fizzled people who gave 0 fucks
Was given up on, so I couldn't give in, rather press my luck, I had refused to let them win
Had to find understanding; I had to comprehend
Searched for a soul, contemplated saving up to buy a heart
Mines priceless; they deemed worthless

Just easy to tear & rip apart

Opted to leave this situation up on a shelf, ironically the situation's sad, it affected my health

Try to pretend, it doesn't bother me

No need to change the locks fuck hiding the key

No one is welcomed in the house that was left unsecured & open

No valuables, no value but useable

Non-disposable baby wiped my eyes, didn't kiss their asses

Cut my losses, define the good, kiss their asses' good-bye

Oh, how they feel like squatting; they be full of shit

I'm pissed

Vacant & broken; left abandoned

Promiscuity

Promiscuity, what could it bring?
It can bring you down, cause you so much pain
The price, the strife
Promiscuity can cause you your life
Be truthful, be honest; be real
How does it make you feel, to bring all the boys to the yard for the deal
& they steal?
You were failed, you got nailed
Promiscuity, robbed you of your soul
So broken, half instead of whole
Rather blame it on your physique, maybe theirs if they're swole
The proof unfolds, it's your physical dad
Couldn't picture being shown love, wanted it so bad
In constant search for affection; left open, so vulnerable with no protection
Trying to fill a void, for empty vessels, never happy you're always sad; now
annoyed with your feelings left destroyed
Promiscuity the promise unkept
You'll end up paying for the lay, with so much regret
A high-end call girl, think check-up; forget a check
A pimp, an owner; just sheer disrespect
Promiscuity suicidal loner
You can't feel yourself too busy fulfilling bonehead's boners

Out of Style

This shit is for the birds, it's been awhile
Searching about, the drought has you
Annoyed filling the void
Dressed up with nowhere to go
The companion & relation ships sailed away
You've souped up, been stood up, now your fed up, there's nothing no one can say
Ripping off your sleeve, your heart has been placed at the bottom of their shoes
Breaking your sole, stringing you along
Treating you wrong, you're all torn apart, your soul worn out
Bell Bottoms tripped over, Apple bottoms bitten
Written all over your face
Rocked the cut off crop top with the lace underneath your
Overalls' graffitied… "I'm over love" attitude
Not feeling round the way, the high low waisted
Bitter you spit love out too salty you tried still taste it
No Kriss kross, no looking backwards
"Damn you" rings loud & your bamboo earrings you've taken off
Just that the feeling remains heavy, value of less cloth
Over feeling cheap & cheated easy to rip
It seems not to last; too tough to grasp, hard to grip
Conform to the high platforms, cautious to catch yourself right before you slip
Began sweating the small stuff, the words I love you rolling off the tongue can't stick because they are slick
You avoid getting heated rather stay cool so your silk don't wet
The "Rays" the son of a bitches you refuse to wake up to; don't understand TLC (tender, love & care), yet constantly try to talk you out of your pajamas & your underwear

The creeps disrupted your beauty sleep
You peep game, it isn't fear
You never were the casual type, you remain cashmere
Love seems it isn't worth the while
Love has gone out of style

Dying

Can't stop crying
I'm dying, I'm dying
To be loved, the feeling
Of being crushed the rush
Unanswered questions; the lust
I'm dying, should I trust?
I must, I'm dying to be loved genuinely
All the given, all the taking
My heart heavy and aching
They keep piercing, penetrating
I'm cracking, be close to breaking
They are breaking my train of thoughts
Trying to break in & steal my heart out the vault
I'm dying, I'm dying
My fault, I thought the lessons I was taught
If only I could comprehend; I'd mend what I missed from the beginning
To open up, I gave love a try for a fucked up ending
The message I received; I replied, I pressed send
Better a emoji cause my emotions I hide deep within, I pretend
I'm dying to be loved

I'm Fine (Two Words)

With a smile on her face, bright eyes shine
With a knife in her back, hardened spine
She'll keep up this act with these two words "I'm fine"
So broken, she feels her heart squeeze
Love to make others laugh so hard, they feel they can't even breathe
She stays joking, it's hard for anyone to believe when little Miss Sunshine's choking
Someway, she always manage to say these two words "I'm fine"; they're subconsciously spoken
She's quite the envy, so many wish
Stands out in a crowd, she isn't hard to miss
So unbelievable behind closed doors, she contemplates slicing her wrist
Can't read her signals, cause your met with a hug & a kiss, kiss; so stuck up in her fantasy "I'm fine" bliss
Although her life is in ruins, she refuses to let anyone see her cry; time after time, it's that same damn reply; "I'm fine"
Wouldn't get by if she had a real friend, that could call her out on her bullshit play & pretend
Hope these questions, "the how are you's & the how have you beens'?"
Isn't answered with these two words one day & result in a tragic end

"Pretty Eyes Overshadowed Tear Jerkers"

All for Chance

Hoping and wishing, so much for luck
Chance be like, "maybe just maybe she'll want me when she sees my truck,"
"A girl like that man, you must have big bucks"
He's contemplating, hesitating, because she looks so intimidating rolling her eyes and her neck
He can't see the ugly within, feels she's a ten, so he disregards the blatant disrespect
A nervous wreck, he's shaking it's clear
Anticipating the connection; rejection is his biggest fear
He wants to win, he'd bet it all to get in
Chance took a gamble, rolled the dice; she's so hot, yet cold as ice, salty as hell with way too much spice
Can't get to close, so out of touch with reality, she's far sighted
Chance took a chance got dissed and slighted
Twenty years later she runs up in his face, thinking he'd be all delighted
Chance wanted an opportunity given to the rest of them, hoping for the day she'd eventually see the best in him
Treated him like Urkel, made Roger go home
He wasn't the cure for the good girl, bad boy syndrome
What are the chances; the reality, her misery
Her loss; now Chance's a boss, looking fly
Looking very successful in his suit in tie
He makes her cold heart smile, when he walks on by
Meanwhile, the other guys just keep passing her around and make her cry
She didn't take a Chance

False See

It's what he want you to see; he steady be flossing
The image he be portraying; money getting, bossing
No stock in estates, relies on baby mamas in different states
She holds the weight; while he never gets hungry and run out of cake
So childish in his ways, enabled for the rest of his days
Claiming the property of his female or his female as property
Producing the new definition of a shemale, wanting to be viewed properly
Ole boy hit a growth spurt when his money got tall
So much trust put into his image, he'd break them down like a wall
Preyed on stupid women, he feared a super woman; he'd impersonate
Superman left what could've been wonderful women; "Wonder Woman",
wondering how & trying to raise a man
They couldn't quite understand, he was living a facade; failed to realize he
should've been king to a queen instead of trying to be her God
His action provides the proof
He's such a false see, so far from the truth

Boys Versus Men

Boys make plays
Men make plans
Boys invest their time playing with toys
Men stock up, they make investments
Boys playhouse
Men commit by turning their girlfriends into their spouse
Boys complain, they think their girl wants everything; they feel she's simply too much
Men value their rib; they don't drool no need for a bib
They understand their women hold them up; they're very beneficial like a crutch
Boys break under pressure, fall apart; they crack
Men carry the weight of their families on their backs
Boys focus on keeping their shoes clean
Men show support for their kid's dream
Boys hide their feelings, go from girl to girl
Men love their queens, they give and make them their world

Mannequin

She's poised, strategically posed
Chin to the ceiling, sense bullshit with her nose
You stare at her, you admire her fit
The store is closed, keep checking the time; can't wait, feel its about to be lit
The door swings open, she lets you in
Seems heartless and cold dressed sharp; the mannequin
You know what's in store, is a front she doesn't see nor feel
Her statue her build, no time for a cheap thrill
Her vibes, she's desensitized, so you shop around, for a bargain looking for a steal
Meanwhile, it never registers what's stored inside, a blank face can't look into her eyes
Lifeless cause her heart was broke and stole
Mannequin so stiff, who'd expect her to have a soul?

Mad Dog

Go around, inflicting pain
Mentally insane, snatching up happiness with your cane
PTSD you try to shake, what will it take?
A drink, some meds, a bullet to the brain
You cry and you beg
"It's my leg", "It's my leg"
Your excuse for not standing up right
Made it through the war, to come home to argue, fuss, and fight
Bitterness has plagued you, grinding your canines ready to dig in to bite
All while wagging your tail
Won't turn the other cheek, keep acting up; gonna wind up dead or in jail
So miserable, you love reeking hell
Mad dog, pitbull, calm down sit
Stop holding grudges; avoid the pit
From all that barking you must refrain
Until then you'll remain, in a fenced in dog house, due to your short chain

Male Function

Get it together, do right
What does the body good?
Glory deemed you necessary, a sight for sore eyes
Yet you have poor vision, think indispensable never discretionary
So what life for you isn't going great, the pain you want badly to escape
Boss up multitask, never feel like it's too much to ask
Focusing on one thing, you're pressed need to de-stress you break
It's ok you've made some mistakes, just work on yourself; never hesitate
Hold onto your faith and the attacks won't work; hope one day you'll be
able to disregard the hurt
You must know when you attempt to fix; your demons will pull, tug, jerk,
& twist
Refuse to stay broken, tore up, out of order; you're only in your prime
Focus and don't step out of line
Don't fall asleep; you can't afford to lose your mind
Malfunctioning not functioning; keep puncturing, your heart bleeds
Avoid being mislabeled; seen as unfit, unstable
You're no displaced manual, for a true woman she'll find you, you won't
be too hard to read
She'll wrap you up, make sure you don't bleed
"Get out," don't get sunken
Think with your head, use your brain, concentrate, just function

Suited

You put on your jacket, every day you give your best
Not dressed to impress for Sunday's
You walk the walk instead of the runways
Custom fitted, tailored made
Could never be low cut; always got your morals up, don't mind rocking a fade
When pressed, never stressed you adjust your cuffs and tie
Stay on top of things, you hold your head up high
No scuffs, your shoes stay polished; can never be worn by some mediocre guy
You handle your business, put in time; receiving more than a check
You focus on your responsibilities as a man, which earns you great respect

Mr. Comfortable

Mr. Comfortable
He didn't want to grow
Mr. Comfortable
So relaxed he failed to show
Mr. Comfortable
Had a temper with no chill
He thought time stood still
Had no drive, no will
His dreams had been killed
No emotions, couldn't feel
He couldn't keep it real
Just pain he would deal
Hard hearted, couldn't heal
Mr. Comfortable
I had to let him go

Love's Prisoner

You gave him the key to your heart
You understand the vow "until death do us part"
The hold that he has on you, makes it hard for anyone to get through
It seems impossible to break, the walls the bars prevent your escape
Confused about what's real, what's fake
Someone who guards you, you protect; what he dishes you just take
Blindsided by love; the bodyguard you connect; the one that holds you
captive, the one who neglects
A glimmer of hope shines through; a moment to retrospect
No more than a officer who'd bring correction, between love and hate
there's a thin line and no affection
A crime of passion, bad thoughts of love, show sympathy cause it's not
perfection
Now you are fully aware that you've been serving time
It's bad that when love is wrong, so you fight for your rights
Only to endure continuous solitary confinement filled with lonely days
and nights
You've come to see clearly your situation
Your freedom hangs in the balance of your imagination
You beg for mercy, hopeful for probation
The key you hold doesn't fit Love's chains
Love's prisoner, prisoner of love shall you remain?

Manipulators

People who play the victim
Who never see the good
Always preaching about something you should do, but never see what they could
Play one excuse after another
Truly understanding, now you're Ms. Understood; miserable and hating their own life
Feel high when they bring you strife
Reading scriptures, acting all holy
To drain and suck the life out of you solely
It's a true story, time tells no tale
You know the truth, cause all they bring you is hell

ICU

Was blind
I Folded
I'm sorry, I'm sorry
Played you like a video game; Atari
Tried to control the controller, wasn't gon let you win
Didn't care if you were waiting to exhale; to simply breathe again
You monitoring every move, me not supporting you wholeheartedly
Now listening to old groves like so sick
Got me feeling blue and lethargic
Unfortunate circumstances, the situation's clear
Clear vision, no clairvoyant, just lacked common sense; but the presence
of death is near
So, hurry without hesitation
Someone please call 911
I was a guest in our home, I was out of line, no connection, left to rome;
just out having fun
You were always hospitable, now i'm pitiful in this hospital
My guess I had it coming, put away my childish ways, no more running
No longer leaving room for you to feel empty and vacant
Don't leave me, I won't be able to take it
Life expectancy, now I know what's expected, I'd been reckless
I lacked support, sorry I had you feeling neglected
Your heart's failure; I've resurrected, showing intensive care
The resuscitation; no coma so I'm fully aware
Had to stop being critical, forgive me for making you hysterical
Give all my heart this time, I swear
My unstable condition; bottom line I fell flat
I need you; I love you
So please come back
I SEE YOU

Fly Trap

To catch a guy, to get a guy
Ladies are told they must look fly
Got to push them up, stick it out
To feel certified and approved when he shouts
A whistle or holla, "looking good shorty" aloud
Suppose to have you walking around proud with your head up in a cloud
Just keep in mind there are many fly honeys that be swarming 'round
Getting caught up and collected by the pound
He isn't trying to keep them away from his plate; he loves when flies stick to him like duct tape
He loves the attention, it makes him feel great
He'll guarantee to be one hundred and promises to keep it real
When a flies' buzzing become aggravating he gets a sudden urge to smash; to kill
He'll surround himself around others to swat and feel
Feeling all honored and such the catch
He's caught up in his own fly trap; can't tell him nothing, he's the shit
So full of himself, of course; he's a flies' main dish

Brainiac

He assumed it was his muscle I was after
I only wanted his brain
All the thirsty chicks stayed lined up
I never focused on being the main
Often felt he was a lame
To protect & shield my heart from pain
I told him not to come, back that ass up, then he made it rain
Over & over again ; time after time, I'd come to lose my mind
He'd taken the long drive downtown, when I'd get lost
he'd seek to surely find
He damn near drove me insane; took me on many trips, he didn't need
a plane
After all that blowing smoke up my ass, found he talked a lot of game
Yes, he was good at using his tongue, could never forget his name
I had to place him in my contact list as "don't answer" when the telephone
would rang

Melination

I once heard a brother; whose mother was of color say that melanin was too strong

I listened at his opinions, he made several attempts to diminish; needed him to hang himself, so I went right along

I let him finish

With charm, I apologized for him being wronged

I hated the fact that he had misunderstood the melination; held my composer, internalized my frustration

He'd been generalizing, despising; he couldn't recognize that he was beaten a sister down like mister; looking all silly

If you could have seen the expression on my face, my thoughts what a disgrace; woah really

His statements of black women always being sour, fight to control, want to take the man's role, stay craving power & are incapable of being sweet

I politely told him his misguided feelings he should never ever-ever; ever-ever repeat

He seemed bitter; the fact that one birth him, didn't unnerve him; since he couldn't resonate with her, I felt he didn't deserve one

Hoped he'd see the revelation, not quite sure what made me ask him had he seen "Birth of a Nation"

Not calling for a revolution but dude was spreading divide & conquer pollution

I managed to stay relaxed; didn't bring out my fist pick; even though, I was hella tight like a fro

Figured I'd go, light on the defense; show restraint, give him my reality then see what he thinks

I'd testify to dispel those slanderous myths

I had to let him know

I mean a man who failed to understand that kindness is a character trait, that I would never consider him a traitor, but I most definitely had to let him know that he was self-inflicted hater

How dare you disrespect the woman that made you

Attitude comes in all shades and sizes, when the melanated queen king is down, she rises; see through the other's disguises realize the lies that makes you despise us

Don't drown black women, because you rather reach inside the cracker jack box to claim prizes

Her struggle, her cries, so foul; how come she's not allowed to swim in her emotions

So sad when she's left to feed her kids through child support negations

Told him, love is not of color; it's just his feelings, his unfortunate circumstances & dealings I'd pray for since "black women" are too strong I'd be honored to do the kneeling

He was quite heavy, it took everything I had in me to lift him up

His head was bowed down, I walked away slightly readjusted my crown

I didn't hear not one sound; my guess I humbled him, his jaw laid on the ground

He got melanated:

She's a queen you see
A Nubian Goddess
When your down, she rises
Made perfectly, in his vision
Don't misuse, don't neglect her
Don't abuse, don't disrespect her
Don't refuse to accept her
A queen you need

Silence

I'm kind-so I choose instead
To kill him with silence
Won't wish him dead
Pre-meditation; "con?" content without malice
The weapon of choice; a deaf ear
For when he grabs his chest and gasp for breath, I simply won't hear
No silencer needed, I won't be using a gun
Plan of attack—catch him off guard, leave him shocked & stunned
Mission to leave no witnesses-no protection
Leave him wounded, open & bleeding; rather run through his blood stream lethal injection
No accident-he's a wreck; best revenge is to do good, he's sure to break his neck
Dug a hole so deep, won't be grinning when it's time to reap
For if he reaches to grab me with his arms, attempts to overpower me with his charm
All the baiting, no negotiating; he won't farewell
I'm the executioner, no deliberating; I simply refuse to live in a beautiful hell
I'll kill him with silence
Crickets the sound-he can cry a mutha-fucking river but I' won't drown
No need for an anchor to hold down
No duct tape, no twisty hog-ties hands & feet free, this dog won't be bound
I'll kill him with silence
Give him a "fuck" to remember, getting me bodied, his body I won't dismember

No trigger, just the middle finger, I ain't bitter; I won't reside in anger
No menace, just reminiscing on contentment right before death's grip-
Watched the clock tick, been ticked; he's expired
Gathered the evidence through it in a bag; took out the trash
Had a good ole laugh; didn't Angela Bassett that ass; no need to set shit on fire
Waited so long to clean up this mess; decided to be the better person didn't stomp & rip his heart from his chest
I ch`o`se to kill him with silence
To save myself and didn't look back, no casings left-left the scene intact
An eye for an eye; naw this was vengeance turned karma
Had to strap up & put on full armor
My broken heart exchanged for a heart; just pay back
I killed him with silence instead of kindness; after all this snake was spineless
He remains unsure, on shore, instead of the ocean floor
I dipped, took my final trip let the ship set sail
I killed him with silence
No need to repent, no solitary confinement, didn't have to skip out on bail
Had to remain free, cause I'm too bright for jail
I'm kind, so I ch`o`se instead- to kill him with silence, to me he's been dead

Enabler

You'd keep me company when you'd pull my panties off
Your hard on hardened me, I use to be so soft
Finding faults and misplacing insecurities
The audacity; the pleas, the apologies
Being mute was of no use despite the lies, pacifying your cries
For some reason, I could never silence the abuse, so I kept questioning why
You dug the hole, I provided the shovel
Started to dis, dismiss, only to end up disheveled
Far from level headed felt a void, the issues avoided; we dreaded, never
resolved; not deaded
Enablement, now hella bent
To resentment, it all happened in a blur
I had to at least accept my part, took responsibility found the cure in order
to restore my peace
I forgave myself in aiding and abetting
Had to let you go; forgiving and forgetting
I was the enabler

Puzzled

Attempt to put together, gather all the pieces on the floor
Scattered about, not knowing what's in store
Start with the corners work your way in
A little frazzled round the edges yet, beautiful skin
Every piece tested coincide to make sure she's a fit
When it's all said and done it's the perfect pic
You rub your hand along the cracks and are careful not to break apart
Cause it's complicated to put back
You stare and admire this breathtaking piece of art
She's speechless trying to search for words like in Ruzzle
You've caught her by surprise; she's puzzled

Kin-Dred

Was on cloud nine, made a bed I would eventually lie in
Lies ran my head; I heard him, he said he sees me
This drowned out my cries of wanting to be
So long longing for my soulmate, I'd settled for a kindred spirit
We vibed, he touched me he didn't have to use his hands, my heart didn't fear it
He filled me up; he was a breath of fresh air, I sang a praise
Nothing like the ex & the expectations of any future baes
I stopped running like the sands of time; I kept in mind, the many nights
I cried and all my unanswered prayers
Finally realized what was hiding underneath the layers
Was so tired of begging someone to please call 911 or a doctor
Kept ghosting was in need of someone to defend me like proctor
I've committed to control, I've submitted to power
God sent me an angel; to untangle me from the bed webbed of lies, before
I grew sour
This influenced my decision, of making the deep incision
I was shocked, he'd jumpstart my heart, I prepared for surgery
He was operating on another level
I was gassed, he wasn't looking to smash, he wasn't looking for ass
Even though, I felt he'd be temporary like a sample booth in a grocery store
I didn't want for much but, I always knew that I deserved more
I let him pass; I couldn't deny him
He wasn't thirsty; I was a sip of tea, spicy cinnamon flava
So with me not being a whore, there was no need for a captain save her
I'd be someone he would forever adore
We related; minus the relations; helped to relieve one another's frustrations
You know it's rare to find someone who actually listens and they do, do
Not pretend like they don't hear shit then swear you're their boo boo
So I was through; no set date, I could patiently wait on my soul mate
So long with longing, I'd sleep good at night not yearning yet yawning
Resting peacefully and snoring; grateful for when I rise even if it's by myself
in the mornings

"Pretty Eyes Wiped Away Her Fears"

Love Rollercoaster

The thrill, the excitement
Hands in the air
The screaming, the yelling
What an up and down loveable affair
The ticket issued, your strapped in; the bars lock
The ride seems to be going stable
Until you reach the top
On cloud nine, then it suddenly drops
Your adrenaline rush, but your heart doesn't stop
You cling and you shout
You continue to ride it on out
Knowing it's too late to get off, you've pressed your luck
Suddenly your thinking "what the fuck"
Your gut instinct, throwing your hands up, can no longer hold it down
You still remain hopeful to seek common ground
Coasting the ride driven by love power
Bold enough to take a risk not becoming bitter & sour
Brace yourself; the requirements for this ride you'll face isn't for cowards

Love Defined

Love is a feeling
Love can bring a rush
Love is more than a secret crush
Love is true
Love is not what you say, but do
Love isn't superficial
Love is unconditional
Love is undying
Love is undenying
Love is forever
Love will never sever

The Couple

A couple of good times
A couple of bad
A couple who focus on being happy, instead of being sad
A couple of tears
A couple of years
A couple who conquers all their fears
A couple of laughs
A couple of cries
A couple who choose truth amongst the lies
A couple that's bound to hold each other down;
and will pull the other up, so the other won't drown
A couple that shows love
A couple that's full of hope
Is "The Couple" that stays afloat

The Wait

One step closer, you contemplate
Afraid of making a huge mistake
Still hunger for a love that's great
You hesitate, you simply just prefer to wait
Been hurt before; experienced a heartbreak
Difficult dealings, love seems unappealing; it isn't a piece of cake
No more wasting your feelings on the fake; tricky situations seriously you
refuse to take
You simply just prefer to wait
For a spirit filled connection found by fate
A mate perfectly for you, God took his time to create
What's the rush, don't intend to alienate
You simply just prefer to wait

Stagnant

Kept me company when you'd come pull my panties off
Your hard on hardened me, I use to be so soft
Kept stroking your ego, flashbacks of the past
Pressed pause, kept wondering how long it would last
Heart locked away in a vault, finding faults & misplacing insecurity
The audacity-I turn up, your volume, where's the value?
Boi please!
Being out of control, the role I'd play in coasting emotional abuse
Motion sickness, easy to call in a truce
I was like quicksand you sunk in quick; what's the use
A concrete rose, didn't wither away & die, after all the cries for help, played
apart in my own demise
The ground wasn't sturdy enough, you dug the hole, I provided the shovel
Began dusting the dirt off my shoulders, started to dis, dismiss, still my
look was disheveled
Rockin bed head, no longer on my level, level not hot & red headed
Old issues were dreaded went unresolved instead of being deaded
I dedicated & sacrificed a bit of my life for you
Dumbo, left looking baffled, dumbfounded like I didn't have a clue
Deemed you complacent, content, comfortable; what was left for me to do?
Stagnant now cognizant, I became true

Let Go

Holding on tight praying to get it right
Plagued by darkness
Can't see the light
Death Grip afraid of falling, scared to slip going in circles, back to the old ways; a roundabout trip
Clinging to the idea of what could be results in rope burned hands blistery, red
The effect; the thoughts run your head
Take a deep breath, relax, & release
In letting go is where you'll find peace

Love Me

Love me lightly, don't love me dark
Love me, love me
Without a heavy heart
Love me when the blue sky is bright
Love me when it turns from day to night
Love me, love me
For keeps, not for play
Love me, love me
In so many ways
Love me endlessly
Love me for a lifetime
Infinitely; definitely beyond
Love me, love me
Love me kind
Love me through the rough & tough times
Love me not just when it's easy
Love me, love me
Don't ever deceive me
Love me when I'm happy
Love me when I'm sad
Love me, love me
Don't treat me bad
Love me gently
Love me sweet
Love me constantly; consistently
Love my flaws
Love my scars
Love me, love me
Beneath the sun, moon, & stars
Whatever you do, just love me

This Skin

A covering so smooth
Yet rough & tough
Stretched & left wrinkled to dry
The soul within this skin cries
The marks, the bruises visible, the melanin
Should only be judged, from what it projections within
The dark spots, the discolorations
Looks ageless, despite hyper pigmentation
Loves to get cuddled & spoiled, welcomes deep massages with baby oil
Use caution, caress this skin softly
Ebony prefers black soap, wouldn't mind Ivory
Should lather with dove, her sensitivity
She break outs; the mold can't hold her in contempt
This skin
The cellulite, the dimples, the busted pimples, holds no resentment trapped
in her pores; open minded not closed
She blushes, her cheeks so rosy; it matches the rosacea on her nose
I suppose it's designed to stay hydrated
This skin
Loves lotion that locks in moisture that deeply penetrates the heart's barrier
& restores healing
After chafing & peeling; it's even more appealing
Mouthwatering about the epidermis
It quenches thirst, grab a bottle or a thermos
This skin will have you all in your feelings; it loves to glow

See Level/The Relating Ship

Let's make love for a lifetime
Stroking one another's ego, easing each other's mind
Life jackets, I suppose
You can be my Jack, I can be your Rose
No see sick just very optimistic
"That's the way love goes" or the saying
Once souls connect & intertwine; they're froze; "I'll never let go", I'm staying no straying
I am yours & you are mine
Should it get heated causing the climate to change things
Sail through the storms & not become estranged, pinky promise to just exchange rings
Surrender, put up the flag, go down, make it easy to slip; to the max I'll climb
Rewind, press pause, catch a grip
I'll look forward to landing, should I trip
Avoid going different latitudes, it's sure to cause gigantic attitudes
Just remember it matters how the captain steers not just what he whips
Let's not go overboard or sink the ship
Same level, we can meet on dock agree & play doc
When coasting along we'll make the boat rock
A toast, cheers to us, cause we'll never stop relating

Reclaim the Max

I'm claiming what's mine
Was given numerous signs
I'm taking back my mind
I gave away too much time
I finally found my spine
I know I'm gonna be fine
Building up my empty heart;
No need for a Valentine's
I promise to stay focused & stay in line
I'm reclaiming my time, reclaiming my mind, reclaiming what's mine to the Max!

Whole Someone

Someone to have
Someone to hold
Someone who makes you laugh
Someone who touches your soul
Someone who's gentle, who's sentimental
Someone who's very smart
Someone who won't break your heart
Someone whom you can trust
Someone who'll keep you as their crush
Someone who consistently makes you smile
Someone who'd go the extra mile
Someone who supports your dreams
Someone who knows there is no "I" in team
Someone nice, someone clean
Someone who says exactly what they mean
That whole someone

Leaf

No direction
Blowing in the wind
Not knowing where you're going
Where will you end?
The breeze, the blows; to & fro
The answer to the question
No one knows
The sun will come out
That's guaranteed
The rain, the watering of the seed
You sprouted from a tough root indeed
Found that life wasn't promising
It's rough; full of facts, it's brutally, honest
Although leaves in the fall, fall
Change is inevitable, you won't remain
You're a leaf blowing in the wind, can't stay the same
Scrapped across the grass, walked on you get crumpled-smashed
Disregarded, raked up, and thrown in the trash
True colors shine through when giving oxygen, so chose to be flexible;
don't break just bend
A little brittle, the unwarranted changes come with the mood of winter
You blow into the doorways, stick to the bottom of shoes
You're left irrelevant with nothing left to prove
You enter your season

The Truth

Lived a lie for so long, made many attempts to right my wrongs
Found refuge in singing songs
Kept signing off key, found my voice & became the keynote speaker
There was no beat that I vibed with
The rhythm was either too fast or slow
My tears made the floor slick
I danced around the real issues; put in my ear piece, prayed for peace but purposefully tuned out truth
Love ballads gave a glimmer of hope, made it a little easy to cope; however, that wasn't enough I began to pray for proof
Truth or dare and I dared no longer to settle
I hungered for truth to slap me in my face; no fancy situation with rose petals
Got good & tired of falling & failing, avoided the pedal stool to learn that love didn't love nobody; everybody plays the fool sometimes
Guarded, hard-hearted; boarded up not letting love in
I rather face dying of thirst; used my tears to wash away all the scuffled marks from being walked on; hoping to eventually face it before being put in a hearse
It was evident, tried to discard the evidence, with no love written all over me, just a dry erase memory
There was no permanent marker, no ink; opted to sit back reflect & think
The hits the pounding, being left dumbfounded; my expectations huh; I wasn't the exception to the rule
Had to rule out the false sees; my answer key was to choose truth every time
Wait for the stars to align, connect the dots, come face to face with one another, have him touch my soft spot
The signal the linguistics, his heart palpitating sending vibrations; the software that only I could understand
I began to realize that truth wasn't an average man
No longer being Ms. Understood, I became to see that truth
Truth came to set me free

So Low/Soul Low/Solo

I use to be so high on life
Somehow, I got knocked down; soul low
Worshipped the ground you walked on
An idol god was crowned
Never meant to take from Jesus, glad I
took some notes
Who were you to feed me dreams to dash them with high hopes
A hopeless romantic is what they say I am
Couldn't make him see what he refused to understand
Hope floats when you're on cloud nine
Always ghosting, lived in his shadow failed to pencil in & read between
the lines
Thought it was late, no soulmate; somehow we were intertwined
To a leach, a soul sucker, an ingrate I was kind
I strengthened up my backbone, then everything was fine
Had to dump him, he was so low; I went solo
I chose to rise & shine

Ocean Floor

Dancing on the ocean floor
The waves roaring
I swirl like seaweed
I twirl like an octopus
Feeling light, I'm exploring
The rhythm and beat swish, swash
I'm left reeling from the waves
They wash, lift, & spin me up to the shore
My movement is smooth, so captivating
My hips back & forth swaying
I flip and flap like a dolphin; I'm a mermaid
I drop, pick it back up; I wiggle, I roll
I dance my tail off
I stroll leaving it all on the ocean floor

Love In The Making

He loves me
The way he makes love to me
He takes his time
The built-up pressure, I'm not easy he helps me to unwind
He touches me deeply, he touches my mind
He finds out all my weaknesses and put them in-line; check
I love how he caresses my neck, reminiscing about how my lips get wet,
from all his tender kisses; those soft little pecks
We're so in tune; my intuition
Wild thoughts, he puts in the key & ignites my ignition
Cause the effect raises my temperature higher, his extinguisher is needed
to put out my fire
The intimacy, the passion stays blazing; he's freakin amazing
The intensity, we get lost he's so far into me
Stroking so wonderfully, my ego lays in a pillow cloud
Shaking stilettos, falsettos vibrating hitting high notes, muffling love
making beautiful music; the pitch is loud
Sending chills & shivers down my spine, he lays claim when he says this
pussy's mine
He's one of a kind, he got me hooked; weak in the knees, legs trembling
from being shooked
I grip tightly, holding on to my buck for dear life, I can't let go
Chopped & screwed; the moment is processed nice & slow
He loves me; to please me is his mission
My river is filled it began to flow; to over run from being placed in a
compromised position
He's such a great lover, I come-unhinged, my damn walls crack,
Making love faces; gazing through his mirrors, our connection reflecting
back, it couldn't be any clearer
I'm finished; I'm done, finally found the one who knows how to make love

Dear Husband

We banded together for life
Branded me with your last name
I'm flashing, brandishing my ring
No more boo thing, I'm your wife
We eat together, we sleep together, we lay together, we should pray together
to weather any storm that arise, to ensure we'll stay together
After all marriage equals compromise
It should only get better, I've quenched your thirst
If you put up, I will shut up, after I yell a lil maybe even curse…so we
don't give up
I'll follow your lead, it's simple just put your woman first
I'm all neck; you are the head
Instead let's try to avoid arguments, I'll give you credit, you are so smart;
you know how they end, you know how they start
Together we can achieve & blow through ceilings
Let's not let the small stuff alter our feelings
So don't take any risk if I'm not feeling all frisky
Let's stay drunk in love no alcohol no whiskey
No temptation, just dedication none of them can match my worth
I'm your girl, I'm your world, I'm your universe
Just remember our vows you said for better or worse
I'd be the candy that causes your toothache, turn right around and fix it
I'd be your sealant
So don't go sulking in your feelings
But just know that if you be my headache, I can make your head ache

But I won't
Cause when we enter the course of action I rather not fake intercourse
So don't
My dear husband make no mistakes, I'm so down to make this marriage great
Signed
Seriously,
Your Loving Wife
P.S.
Can you take out the trash, remember to put the toilet seat down, put your dirty clothes inside the hamper instead laying them all around. I'll do that thing you like…I'm down; kiss, kiss smooches!

Heroine

I dreamt he said...
Heroine, you're like a drug, you're so addicting; I've become addicted
Thoughts of you make me smile, I'm fixated on the way you make me feel
Heroine, please save me, save me; you're so brave
I depend on you so I won't cave
Rescue me from my pain, take away my cares and all my fears; I'll wrap you tight in my arms
You awaken me, you're my alarm; for a piece of you I turn up the charm
You are my shooting star
Heroine, relieve me take me far
You're blazing, got me dazing; purple hazing
You amaze me, **Heroine** you drive me wild, you make me crazy
But a hit, a dose, of you is like a shot to the brain; the anticipation, blood rushes through my veins
You blowout, you make me pop; you take away my breath, you make my heart stop
You pierce my skin and run through my system deeply; withdrawals make it hard, so woke, far from being sleepy
Without you I'd struggle to survive, on you I rely; you got into my head, if you leave, I'd die
I can't deny, I lie craving and shaking in bed
Heroine, you are my fix; methadone couldn't cure this kind of sick
I fear being alone, you are my end; my medicine
When I feel like giving up, I just give into you
Please, don't let me die!

Printed in the United States
By Bookmasters